ALL BRUGGE

10th Edition, July 1991

I.S.B.N. 84-378-0392-6

Dep. Legal B. 25828-1991

GENERAL DISTRIBUTOR FOR BELGIUM: n.v. Van Mieghem A. Editions
Marconistraat 5 (Industriepark) 8400 Oostende
Tel.: 059/70.86.22 - 80.32.95 - FAX: 059/70.10.53

Impreso en España - Printed in Spain
F.I.S.A. Palaudarias, 26 - 08004 Barcelona

Brugge

INTRODUCTION

This book is designed as a lasting memento of one of the most attractive cities in the world: Brugge. Handsome patrician houses, impressive churches and exquisite works of art are the quiet testimonials of its glorious past.

This past is regularly re-lived in ceremonious festivities and processions, which cannot fail to make an unforgettable impression on their spectators.

Brugge, however, is far from slumbering in the shadow of its own past.

Surrounded by half a dozen active and dynamic suburban municipalities, the old town centre is like the beating heart of a living modern community. A responsible and sustained restoration programme has brought the best out of its many buildings and succeeded in filling them with new life.

The sea, to which Brugge owes its origin and its blossoming period in the middle ages, has once more played a major role since the turn of the century. Zeebrugge on the North Sea coast has developed into a harbour of worldwide stature. Visitors here will be astounded by the hum of activity peculiar to a large sea-port, and fascinated by the typical atmosphere in and around the fishing — and yacht-harbours. Numerous recreation facilities, and a pleasant safe beach afford ample opportunities for exercise, relaxation, or a beneficial rest. We may recommend you the many inviting restaurants and other eating-places with charm and atmosphere, which are to be found in Brugge and its surroundings; lovers of good food are sure to appreciate the excellent local cuisine, consisting of several expertly prepared fish and meat dishes.

Brugge is a town in which you can enjoy life to the full.

Belfry or Halles Tower, a unique Flemish building, 13th-15th century.

FROM THEN UNTIL NOW

The destiny of Brugge has always been closely linked to the sea. A first settlement grew up, in fact, round one of the mouths which was carved out by the North Sea between the 4th and 7th centuries. In 862 Baldwin «of the Iron Arm» abducted Judith, daughter of the French King Charles the Bald. The latter found himself obliged to send his rather unwelcome son-in-law to the district of Flanders, to defend it against the increasingly aggressive Normans, who had established a «Bryggja» or mooring-place for their ships at the mouth of the Zwin. It is otherwise generally accepted that the old Norse word «Bryggja» is the origin of the present-day name of Brugge.

The citadel or «castrum» which Baldwin erected gradually developed into a town centre, and in 875 the name of Brugge was mentioned for the first time in a chronicle.

In the course of the 10th century a trading settlement or «portus» involved in the immediate neighbourhood of the castrum, and this contributed to the extensive growth of Brugge and Flanders.

In about 1127 the various settlements became merged into one connected district, which was surrounded by canals. Charles the Good was murdered in this same year, and the tradesmen of Brugge obtained the right to participate in the administration of the town, by the election of aldermen. In this process, Brugge developed from a military fortification into a town of international importance whose power kept pace with an unhindered growth of trade.

The silting of the Zwin, Brugge's outlet to the sea, which commenced during this period, was taken in hand with the founding in 1180 of the out-port of Damme; this town was joined to Brugge by a canal. Commerce and industry, particularly the cloth trade, made 13th century Brugge one of the most populated and prosperous cities in Europe. A smouldering feud between the powerful merchants, supported by the French king, and the less prosperous guild-members, with the Count on their side, finally flared up in 1302 with the «Matins of Brugge» and the subsequent Battle of the Golden Spurs, in which the heir to the French throne suffered an unexpected defeat.

This struggle for power, which resulted in the guilds and trades earning a voice for themselves in the administration of the town, nevertheless did not prevent the 14th century from becoming a golden age in the history of Brugge. As a wool mart, seat of the Hanseatic towns and a world market represented by 17 nations, Brugge exercised an irresistible attraction upon merchants, bankers, and all kinds of artists.

In the same century, as a result of the marriage of Margaret van Male with Philip the Bold, the Burgundian age was ushered in, and Brugge became the centre of a sumptuous court life. Magnificent festivities, tournaments, jousting and exquisite artistic creations were part of the expression of this pomp and splendour; yet even they could not stem the threatening tide of decay. The Zwin became silted beyond hope and Antwerp, which was now rising into the ascendancy, emerged as a rival to Brugge whose claims could not be gainsaid.

After the death of Charles the Bold and Maria of Burgundy, Brugge fell into Austrian hands, despite the valiant resistance of its inhabitants which Maximilian of Austria finally extinguished in 1488. Antwerp, meanwhile, had made capital out of this situation, and gained enormously in importance. For some time, Brugge continued to live on her former reputation, but in the 17th and 18th centuries, after the final closure of the Zwin as a trade route, she was forced to accept a minor role.

In 1794, under the French regime, Brugge became the administative centre of the Department of the Leie; it was after 1815, under Dutch rule, that this district became known as West Flanders.

The end of the century brought a turning-point, thanks largely to the opening of the sea-port of Zeebrugge in 1907. Georges Rodenbach's novel «Bruges la Morte» was one of many influences which began to attract visitors to Brugge, and these pioneers so to speak laid the foundations for Brugge as one of the most prominent touring centres of Belgium and Western Europe.

Its many monuments, buildings and works of art have miraculousy survived two world wars virtually intact, and thanks also to a sensible policy of restoration Brugge is to this day an incomparable town where present and past still go harmoniously hand in hand.

A TOWN TO EXPLORE!

The best place to begin your tour of discovery is the Market Square, where the Belfry literally and figuratively sets the tone.

You will experience a sense of enchantment when the 47 bronze bells start to ring out from the belfry. Throughout the centuries the belfry has pealed out glad tidings and messages of happy events; and some of its tidings, too, have been of sad, sombre and deathly import.

The town statutes, which were announced from the balcony of the Belfry, earned the name of «Orders of the Halles». The Halles, which together form a whole with the Belfry, served for many years as a market place. In fact, every Saturday morning the weekly market day takes place on the Market Square — a tradition dating back to the year 958.

The Provincial Hof (Provincial Court) is also impressive. Until 1787 it was the Water— or Cloth-Halles; the building arches over the canal from which the flat-bottomed barges, laden to the brim with Flemish cloth, used to set off for the out-ports, to return with foreign wares of all kinds.

Most of the buildings round the Market Square have played an important role in Brugge's history. Among them can be seen the former guild-houses with their typical stepped gables: «Craenenburg» House, where Maximilian of Austria spent some disagreable days in captivity; and «Boechoute» House, from which the town magistrature used to observe the festivities on the Market.

The statue in the centre of the square which represents Jan Breydel and Pieter de Coninck bears witness to the struggle for emancipation of the members of Brugge's guilds and crafts between 1302 and 1304.

Belfry or Halles Tower by night.

Brugge's most important monument, the Belfry and its Halles, forms an impressive whole which reflects the glory of the town's past by day and night. In olden days all the inhabitants of Brugge were summoned from this tower to gather on the Market Square beneath.
The town's statutes earned the name «Orders of the Halles» by virtue of their being announced from the balcony of this building.

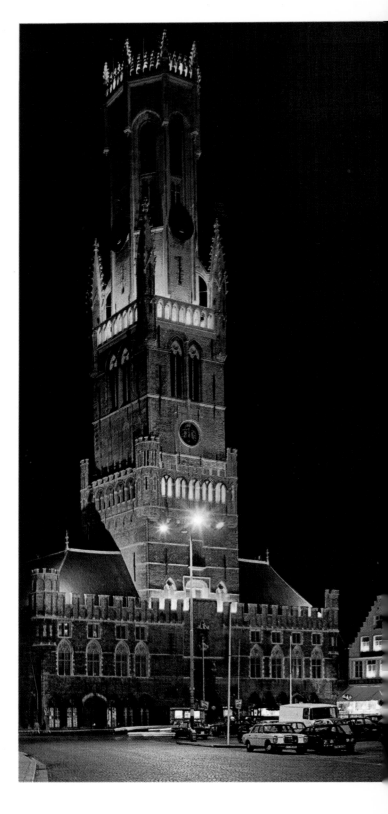

Victory Bell.

On the 220th step of the Belfry or Halles Tower, the visitor can glimpse the famous «Victory Bell», with a diameter of 2.05 m. This bell is only rung on very exceptional occasions.

Carrilloneur at the keyboard.

Although the tones produced by the belfry's automatic mechanism are a pleasure to the ear, they cannot rank in purity of sound and tone with the music played on the keyboard.

After climbing the 366 steps of the 83 meter high Belfry and Halles you will be rewarded with a magnificent view. The belfry mechanism can also be visited on your way up: it consists of 47 bronze bells weighing 27 tons in all. The mechanism is in three separate parts:
1. The bells
2. The keyboard
3. The automatic mechanism
You reach the machine room and drum after mounting the 333rd step. The belfry's automatic mechanism consists of a massive copper cylinder, called a drum, which is 2.5 metres long and 2.06 metres in diameter. It is the largest in existence, weighs 9,000 kg. and has 30,500 openings.
Adjustable steel pins can be inserted in the openings so that in the course of rotation they come into contact with the steel staves and levers which operate the bell-clappers. The belfry keyboard is situated 19 steps higher. When playing this instrument the carrilloneur sets the clappers in motion by striking the keyboard which is connected to them by a set of steel staves and levers. The belfry keyboard is played with hands and feet and requires great physical effort on the part of the carrilloneur.
In order to operate the heavier bell-clappers the player has to stamp the pedals with his feet.

Photo detail and roof architecture of Provincial Court —
19th century.

MECHANISM
of the carillon

KEYS

KEYBOARD

PEDALS

DRUM

AUTOMATIC SYSTEM

E. UTEN

Photo detail.
Front gable Provincial Court — 19th century.

Market Square.

Statue of Jan Breydel and Pieter de Coninck — popular heroes and freedom-fighters (1302-1304), erected in their honour in 1887. In the background, the 19th century Provincial Court.
A number of other historic buildings can be seen on the Market Square. A house with a 15th century gable on the corner of the St. Amandstraat is topped with a compass-card. Opposite stands «Craenenburg» House where Archduke Maximilian of Austria was held prisoner in 1488 when the populace rebelled against his government.
Several houses on the Market Square used to belong to the guilds, and some of them still display the symbol of their history in their architecture: the gable of the weavers' guild house is crowned with a basket, and the date 1621 shows when work began on the fishermen's guild house.

Via the Breidelstraat, with the town archives whose oldest charters date back to the end of the 13th century, you come to the Burg where in 864 the first county stronghold was erected as a defense against the Normans.
Here the eye is rewarded with something in the nature of an architectural anthology. The lower chapel of the Basilica of the Holy Blood is in Romanesque style; the Town Hall is Gothic; the Old City Clerk's Office (Griffie) is Renaissance; the Law Court is classical and the Deanery (Proosdij) Baroque.

The Burg.

The Burg is approached via the Breidelstraat. Various handsome old buildings merit attention here: the Law Court (18th century); the Town Clerk's Office (Griffie) (16th century) and the Town Hall, which saw successive alterations and enlargements during the 16th and 17th centuries and whose front gable dates from the 14th to 15th century.
Adjacent to the town hall on the right is the Basilica of the Holy Blood (12th to 16th century), only part of which is visible in this picture. Its beauty is reflected in greater detail later in this book.
All these buildings are open to the public, and their interior architecture as well as their carefully preserved centuries' old art treasures can be admired.

The Town Hall, whose foundation stone was laid by Louis van Male in 1376, is one of the earliest examples of the typical building style of Brugge which has become so famous. 48 window-recesses, contained between upper and lower windows, together with the small conical towers that crown the building, accentuate a pronounced verticalism.

From the balcony of the Town Hall, where the first States General of the Netherlands gathered in 1464, the Counts of Flanders used to swear their oath affirming respect of the civic liberties.

The Gothic Hall, situated on the first floor, is particularly remarkable for its magnificent wooden ceiling and its colourful historical frescoes.

The Old City Clerk's Office (Griffie), built in Flemish

The Town Hall of Brugge is recognized as the oldest in the Netherlands. Photo detail of front gable.

Photo detail of the former Deanery of Saint Donatian's — 17th century Baroque style with statue of Dame Justice.

Town Hall — the Gothic Room.
Restoration work has included the historical frescoes at the end of the 19th and beginning of the 20th century. The artistically carved ceiling is authentic and belongs to the end of the 14th and beginning of the fifteenth century, as also the original mural decorations which have since disappeared.

Basilica of the Holy Blood (12th-16th century). Visitors to this sanctuary will appreciate that the building consists of two chapels. On the ground floor is Saint Basil's Chapel (the Crypt); above it is a second chapel in which the relic of Christ's Blood is preserved. The basilica also houses a museum containing several distinctive works of art.

Renaissance style (1534-37), has served in turn as the Town Clerk's Office, the Police Headquarters (after the French Revolution), and as the Justice of the Peace's Office (since 1883).

The Law Court (1722-27), built in classicist style, is well worth a visit, not least on account of its artistically carved Mantelpiece of the «Brugse Vrije» in honour of Emperor Charles after his victory over the French King François I in the Battle of Pavia (1525).

The Deanery (Proosdij), dating from 1662, where the deans of St. Donatian's Cathedral formerly exercised control and jurisdiction over their domains, is a handsome testimonial to the Baroque style. Under the trees next to the Deanery, you can with a little imagination visualize the former majestic St. Donatian's Cathedral. This sanctuary, built in about 900, the burial place among others of Jan Van Eyck and Juan Luis Vives, was demolished under the French regime in 1799; St. Saviour's Cathedral replaced it as the town's main church. A stone maquette gives a good idea of the original appearance of this impressive building.

Basilica of the Holy Blood.

Saint Basil's Chapel (the Crypt).

This chapel, or Crypt, was built in the 12th century by Diederik van den Elzas, Count of Flanders. The Saint Basil's Chapel or Crypt has kept its original form and is the only Romanesque building of its kind in West Flanders. An incomparable effect is achieved by the simplicity of the interior and by the stunning bareness of the walls of the three brick aisles. Throughout its splendid past the Crypt served as the Counts' chapel, the Companions' oratory, the Guilds' temple and the Councillors' court of justice. In this chapel is preserved the beautiful 14th century masterpiece of Our Lady of Charity, also known as the Pietà. The Ecce Homo statue can also be seen here: a great work of art and an unrivalled piece of wood-carving. Behind a cast-iron grille you may glimpse part of the original small round tiles of the authentic floor-work.

The Basilica of the Holy Blood consists of two chapels built one over the other. The lower is the St. Basil's Chapel, founded in 1150 by Diederik van den Elzas as the count's chapel. It was the original infrastructure of the Romanesque upper chapel, which has been rebuilt since the 15th century into a more spacious church in Gothic style. The relic of the Holy Blood is preserved in this upper chapel. The magnificent original stained-glass windows, destroyed during the French Revolution, were first replaced in 1845; and once again, after a bomb explosion in 1967, they were restored by the painter De Loddere of Brugge.

Pietà (Crypt).

Altar of the Precious Blood.

Ecce Homo (Crypt).

The upper chapel is a treasury of works of art: paintings, carvings, the work of gold — and silversmiths, a marble altar, and a wooden pulpit in the form of a terrestrial globe, sculpted in the 18th century by H. Pulincx.

The great attraction in the museum of the basilica is undoubtedly the reliquary shrine, the work of Jan Crabbe, executed in gold and silver, and decorated with precious stones.

According to tradition the relic of the Holy Blood was brought to Brugge at the time of the Second Crusade, having been venerated in Constantinople. Every year in May, on Ascension Day, the Procession of the Holy Blood files through the decorated streets of the town. The shrine of the Holy Blood is unquestionably the most valuable treasure preserved in the museum of the Chapel of the Holy Blood: it is made of gold and silver encrusted with precious stones, the work of Jan Crabbe (17th century).

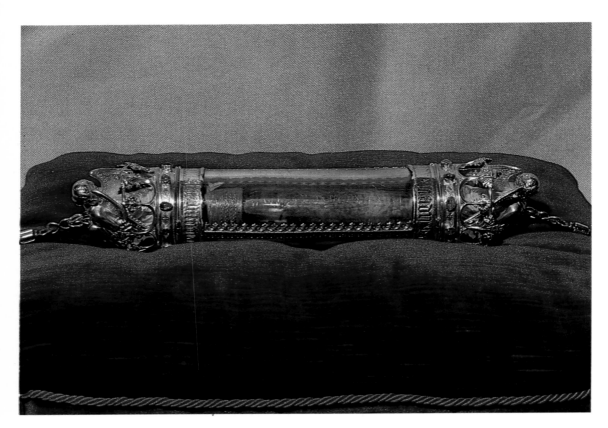

The relic of the Holy Blood.

High altar: "Last Supper" in alabaster (16th century).

Stained-glass window (Basilica of the Holy Blood).

City Clerk's
Office
(Griffie) —
16th-century
Flemish
Renaissance
style — now
the Justice
of the
Peace's
Office.

*Huidenvet-
tersplein —
in the centre
a restored
column
whose
emblem is
connected
with the
cobblers'
trade.
Number 10
on this little
square is the
17th century
«Clobblers'
Guildhouse».*

Rozenhoedkaai and Belfry — top right: 17th century Tanners' House (Huidenvettershuis).

Walking through the Blinde Ezelstraat towards the tavern of the same name which must always have stood there, you will see the Fishmarket and the Huidenvettersplaats with the old tanner's craft-house, before coming out onto the Rozenhoedkaai, a picturesque corner which is sure to arouse your romantic imagination. The lofty spire of Our Lady's Church is already visible in the distance.

Wollestraat with Belfry and (right) old patrician house.

The Dijver.

Along the Dijver at night.

*Church of
Our Lady.*

Stroll along the Dijver past the buildings of the College of Europe, and turn in left to the Groeninge Museum. This Municipal Museum of Fine Arts, built in the grounds of the old Eeckhout Abbey, contains an exceptionally rich collection of paintings by the so-called Flemish Primitives. Among the works on view here are masterpieces by Jan van Eyck, Rogier van der Weyden, Gerard David, Hugo Van der Goes and Jan Memling. Also represented are the most important artistic trends up to and including the contemporary masters. The «Imaginary Van Eyck Museum» is a splendid addition to what can be seen here: a room in which a collection of remarkably well produced colour slides of different sizes is displayed gives an excellent panorama of the work of this great Flemish painter.

Brugge, Groeninge Museum.
«The tithing» (1620) — detail — Pieter Bruegel jr.
(1564-1638).

Photographic archive, Groeninge Museum.
Photographer: M. Platteeuw, Brugge.

Brugge, Groeninge Museum.
«The Preaching of Saint John the Baptist» — Pieter
Bruegel jr. (1564-1638).

Brugge, Groeninge Museum.
«The Baptism of Christ» — Gerard David (✝ 1523).

Photographic archive, Groeninge Museum. Photographer: M. Platteeuw,
Brugge.

Brugge, Groeninge Museum.
«Philip the Good» — Rogier Van der Weyden (copy) 2nd
half.

Photographic archive, Groeninge Museum. Photographer: M. Platteeuw,
Brugge.

Brugge, Groeninge Museum.
«The Moreel Triptych» (1484) — Jan Memling (†1494).

Photographic archive, Groeninge Museum. Photographer: M. Platteeuw, Brugge.

Brugge, Groeninge Museum.
«Death of the Virgin» — Hugo Van der Goes (†1482).

Photographic archive, Groeninge Museum. Photographer: M. Platteeuw, Brugge.

Brugge, Groeninge Museum.
«The Virgin with the canon» — Jan Van Eyck († 1441).

Photographic archive, Groeninge Museum. Photographer: M. Platteeuw,
Brugge.

Brugge, Groeninge Museum.
«The last Judgment» — Hiëronymus Bosch (†1516).

Photographic archive, Groeninge Museum. Photographer: M. Platteeuw,
Brugge.

Typical upper part of the entrance to the Gruuthuse Museum, seen from the inner courtyard.

Fairytale view of inner courtyard of Gruuthuse Museum at night.

Turning left as you leave the museum, you enter a peaceful green oasis in the heart of the town, namely the Arents Court (Hof Arents). Here you will find the Arentshuis, which is also a museum, housing three different collections: etchings and watercolours which the English artist Frank Brangwyn bequeathed to his native city Brugge, a valuable collection of porcelain, pewter and earthenware, recently donated (1977) to the town by Miss Herssens of Hamme/Sint-Niklaas, and finally a series of remarkable oil-paintings of the town in former times.

In the glass window displays opposite the Arentshuis there is an admirable exhibition of coaches and sleds used in the olden days. The quaint little Bonifacius Bridge and the bust of the Spanish humanist Juan Luis Vives meet you on your way to the inner court-yard of the Gruuthuse Palace.

The Lords of Gruuthuse, who once lived in this

Gruuthuse Museum — mounted statue of Louis van Gruuthuse.

15th century look-out tower of the Gruuthuse Museum, with ornate roofing.

palace, had the sole right of sale of the «gruut», a blend of dried plants used in the spicing of beer. One of the most famous scions of this family was certainly Louis van Gruuthuse, who proclaimed the motto «Plus est en Vous» in his coat of arms. He was a capable diplomat, politician and warrior in the service of the Dukes of Burgundy. During his extremely active life he organized, among other things, many tournaments, extended a generous refuge to the exiled English King Edward IV (1471), and amassed an outstanding collection of books and miniatures which can still be admired in the Bibliothèque Nationale in Paris.

The palace now serves as a museum, where a most varied patrimony is on exhibition: lace, coins, tapestries, musical instruments, weapons, furniture, kitchen equipment and so on. There is also a stone museum with tombstones and archaeological findings on display.

Gruuthuse Museum. General view of the kitchen.

Surroundings of the Gruuthuse Museum.
Inner courtyard of the Gruuthuse Museum with (upper right) part of the adjacent 12th century Church of Our Lady.

The entire group of buildings is dominated by the spire of Our Lady's Church, which ranks in majesty with the tower of the Belfry. Paul Spaak described the two towers as follows, seeing them at sunset linked, as it were, by a golden band:

Vainement le soleil couchant tissa d'orfroi
La tour de Notre Dame et le front du Beffroi.

The Madonna and Child by Michelangelo, sculpted in white marble, is one of the gems of the unusually rich art collection belonging to the church. It is also one of the rare works by this great artist which can be viewed outside Italy. Also of exceptional interest are the splendid monumental tombs of Maria of Burgundy and Charles the Bold; the prayer tribune of the Lords of Gruuthuse; and the choir with the coats of arms of the knights who attended the 11th chapter of the Golden Fleece here in 1468.

Garden of the Arents house — Bridge of St. Boniface.

St. Boniface Bridge — and the church of Our Lady (13th-15th centuries).

Michelan-gelo. White marble statuette (1503-1504) — Madonna and Child. On view in the Church of Our Lady.

Church of Our Lady. Main altar and organ.

Mausoleums of Mary of Burgundy and Charles the Bold.

Tomb with frescoes.

Saint John's Hospital: on the right the entrance of the Memling Museum; on the left a magnificent arch in which the death and coronation of the Virgin are represented.

The Saint John's Hospital stands in the shadow of Our Lady's Church. It is one of the oldest hospices in Europe. Since the second half of the 12th century it has served not only as a hospital, but also as a lodging for travellers. In one of the old wards, a number of Jan Memling's finest works are on view. The jewel of the collection is «The Mystical Marriage of Saint Catherine»; «Sybilla Sambetha», «Martin Van

Saint John's Hospital — inner courtyard.

Saint John's Hospital — part of the oldest buildings.

Nieuwenhove», the «Pièta», «The Adoration of the Magi» and the «Saint Ursula Shrine» have also enraptured countless visitors.

Memling, who was of German origin, after spending periods in Cologne and Brussels, settled definitively in Brugge, where he became a Free Master of Saint Luke's Guild in 1467. A rather more poetic though not altogether verifiable account of his life tells how he was wounded at the Battle of Nancy while serving Charles the Bold as a mercenary soldier. According to this legend, he bequeathed a number of his masterpieces to the Saint John's Hospital in recognition of the good treatment he received there.

The Saint John's Hospital was built in the 12th century, and until 1977 it was one of the oldest active hospitals in Europe. Until 1634 the hospital was run by two orders of monks and nuns. The nuns continued to carry out their duties until 1977, when the hospital was transferred to a modern building on the outskirts of the town. Victims of the plague in times of epidemic were taken into the lower rooms along the water's edge. The hospital's old pharmacy is a very realistic museum in which the ceramic and metal mixing-vessels used in olden times have been carefully preserved and stored in beautifully carved wooden cupboards. Jan Memling's masterpieces are housed and may be seen in the same buildings of the Saint John's Hospital. They are the works of a truly refined spirit which has penetrated into the deepest secrets of the art of painting.

Hans Memling (1433-1494) The Virgin Mary with the Apple.

◁ The shrine of St. Ursula — Hans Memling.

Hans Memling. The Mystic Betrothal of St. Catherine (detail).

Walplaats with spire of Church of Our Lady.

Do not leave the Saint John's Hospital without visiting the Old Apothecary, the Guardian's Room and the Convent Chapel.

As you cross the Maria Bridge, you will notice one of the many «godshuizen» or almshouses which are a characteristic feature of the town: in this case, the «Rooms Couvent». These institutions were placed by wealthy families or trade associations of Brugge at the disposal of the aged and needy.

Turning right through the narrow Stoofstraat and crossing the Walplaats, where in sunny weather you can watch the lacemakers deftly plying their bobbins, you come to the Beguinage.

Lacemakers of Brugge.

This is virtually a miniature town within a town, where time seems to have stood still. In 1299, approximately a century and a half after its foundation, it was raised by Philip the Fair to the stature of a Princely Beguinage, and thus ceased to come under the jurisdiction of the town. But the history of the Beguinage has not always presented a rosy picture: it was ravaged in turn by flood, fire, iconoclasm and the French Revolution. The place of the beguines, who belong to the past as far as Brugge is concerned, has been taken by the Benedictine Sisters, who still wear a garb reminiscent of the 15th century inhabitants of the cloister.

You can get a good idea of the former life-style of the beguines by visiting the typical little house next to the entrance.

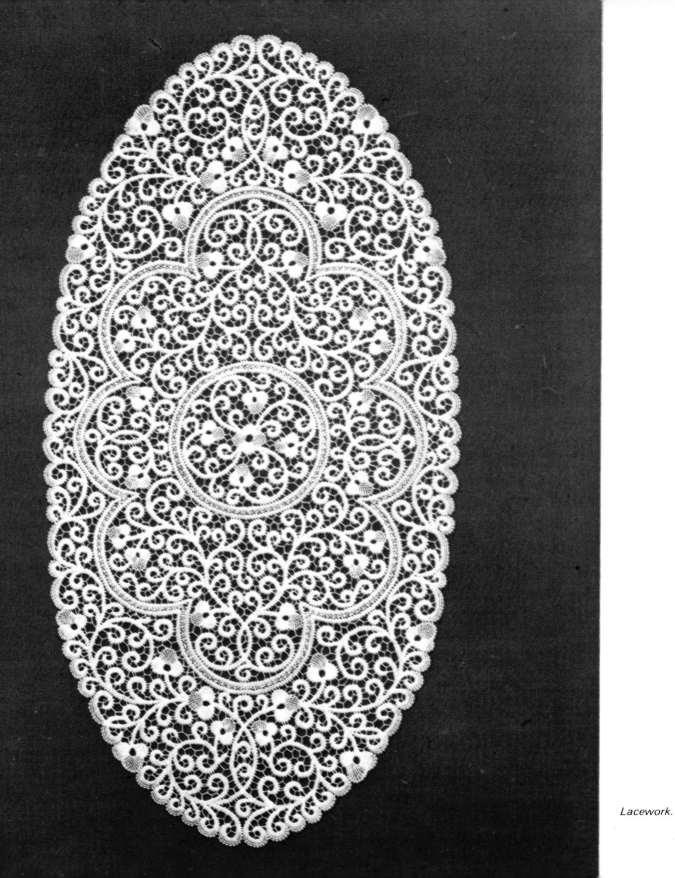

Lacework.

Bridge and entrance to the Princely Beguinage «Ten Wijngaarde».

The buildings of the old Beguinage, situated at the water's edge, date back to the 13th century. The Beguinage developed with the entry into it of girls from all social backgrounds who dedicated themselves to a mystical community life, under the leading of a superintendent called the Grand Mistress.
The Beguinage is undoubtedly the most peaceful spot in Brugge. Nowadays the same Beguinage is still open to those who choose to withdraw for a quiet retreat from our intensely active society, to find peace through devotion and prayer.

Princely Beguinage «Ten Wijngaarde» — beguinal church consecrated to Saint Elizabeth.

Princely Beguinage «Ten Wijngaarde».
The Chapter-House.

Another pleasant sight along the canals and their green
banks are the swans of Brugge. Their decorative forms
unconsciously reflect the attractiveness of the town.

Princely Beguinage «Ten Wijngaarde». Entrance gate seen
from inside.

Brugge is a Mecca for many artists who cannot resist her
picturesque combination of architectural wealth and
natural beauty.

Princely Beguinage «Ten Wijngaarde». Peaceful interior
courtyard of a beguinal house with well.

Princely Beguinage «Ten Wijngaarde».
Place of modesty and peace.

In the close neighbourhood of the Beguinage lies the romantic Minnewater lake. It is difficult nowadays to imagine the hum of activity connected with the loading and unloading of the many vessels which used to drop anchor here.
Swans now glide noiselessly over the water, like white-rigged sailing-boats to whom shipwreck is unknown.

Princely Beguinage «Ten Wijngaarde».
Inner courtyard.

Minnewater with Sluice House (16th century). Spire of Church of Our Lady in the background.

Minnewater.

Tower of Saint Saviour's Cathedral (12th to 13th century).

Retracing your steps along the Wijngaard, Katelijne and Heilige Geest streets, you reach the Saint Saviour's Cathedral.

This building has slowly evolved since the 9th century into a Gothic whole such as it is today (with the exception of the Romanesque base of the tower, which dates from about 1200).

Inside the church, the visitor's eye is immediately drawn to the magnificent pulpit constructed by H. Pulincx jr. in 1785, and to the technically and artistically splendid organ which has provided pleasure for countless music lovers.

Various trades, such as the cobblers and coachmakers, had their own chapels within this sanctuary.

As in the Church of Our Lady, the Order of the Golden Fleece held one of its chapters here in 1478. The small carved wooden figures on and under the arm-rests of the choir, which was constructed to commemorate the above chapter, are individual works of art.

Saint Saviour's Cathedral is in fact much older; it was built in the 9th century and has on more than one occasion been the victim of fire. This sanctuary was raised to the stature of a cathedral in 1834, and prides itself on being the oldest brick building in Belgium. It contains numerous treasures, bequeathed and endowed during its long history, or forming an integral part of the whole, such as: the sculpture of the Creator by A. Quellin (1682); the main choir, decorated with the coat-of-arms of the Knights of the Golden Fleece; the magnificent stained-glass windows; richly woven tapestries and monumental tombs which testify to its glorious past. A valuable collection of paintings by Flemish masters can be seen in the Saint Saviour's Cathedral museum; these works are all perfect of their kind, and seem to have been painted by angelic hands.

Saint Saviour's Cathedral. Main choir.

The church's art patrimony consists further of several remarkable paintings, the majestic high altar flanked by two late Baroque monumental tombs of former bishops of Brugge, and a number of valuable tapestries. The adjoining museum contains in addition to paintings by Dirk Bouts, Pieter Pourbus and Adriaan Isenbrant a considerable amount of precious gold and silverwork, sculpture and embroidery.

Notice, too, as you leave the cathedral the little passion-house where a dramatic Christ figure is seen kneeling in front of the cross. Entering the Steenstraat, keen shoppers are sure to feel their hearts beating a little faster. Together with the Noordzandstraat which runs parallel to it, this street is undeniably one of the shopping paradises of Brugge. The choice of goods in the shops, ranging from sophisticated boutiques to well-stocked supermarkets, is appealing to every taste.

Under the gaze of the statue of Simon Stevin, the famous Dutch scientist who was born here, a colourful flower market is also held here on Saturday mornings.

Proof of the fact that trading establishments are not merely interested in profit is the very successful restoration of a pair of gabled store-fronts, carried out largely at the owners' own cost.

In the meantime we have made our way back to the Market, where a delicious cup of coffee or a frothing pint of beer make a nice way to round off a preliminary acquaintance with the old town of Brugge.

Saint Saviour's Cathedral. 17th century organ loft and 18th century organ.

Saint Saviour's Cathedral. Choir.

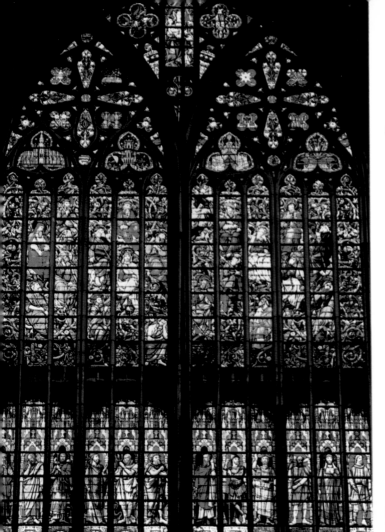

St. Saviour's Church - stained-glass window.

St. Saviour's Cathedral.

Saint Saviour's Cathedral. Early 18th-century bronze door under the organ loft.

If this first reconnaissance of Brugge has whetted your appetite, you will find the Market Square a good starting-point for a second tour of exploration.

The Vlamingstraat, where various financial institutions are no accidental reminder of the economic activity which characterized this district, leads you straight into the old «Hanseatic Brugge».

The square now occupied by the Municipal Theatre housed for a number of years (1468-78) the «Platform of Liège» (Luikse Perron), a freedom symbol of that fiery town which was transferred here by Charles the Bold as a punishment to the rebellious inhabitants of Liège.

On the right of the theatre stands the «Nation House of Genoa». Two other Italian Nation Houses, those of Florence and Venice, which have since disappeared, used to be situated in the immediate neighbourhood.

Merchants gathered here, stored their wares here and established their consulates on this spot.

Although Brugge cannot lay claim to a stock exchange, or bourse, she was instrumental in the origin of the name: in front of the Huis Ter Buerze, which was once the home of the Van der Buerze family, merchants used to carry out all kinds of business such as the exchange of money and so forth, in just the same way as this is still done in the established stock exchanges of the world's major cities.

The Academiestraat, embellished by various attractive Renaissance gables, leads you into a square dominated by the statue of Jan Van Eyck and surrounded by impressive buildings.

The Porters' House (15th century).

Spiegelrei with former Porters' Lodge (15th century) in the background: now the State Archives.

The Porter's Lodge was a gathering-place and relaxation centre for prominent porters. The name «porter» did not refer to someone living within the city gates, though it originates from the term «portus». In a niche of the building, which serves at present as the Royal Archives, the «Little Bear of Brugge» proudly stands. During certain festivities it is often dressed up in different costumes.

The bear, which also appears in the town's coat-of-arms, seems to have been the first living creature that Baldwin of the Iron Arm met in this hitherto inhospitable terrain about 11 centuries ago.

The Old Toll House, which is now the Municipal Library, and the Pijndershuis next door to it are another reminder of the busy trade which was once carried on here. The Lords of Luxembourg used to exact a toll on the ship's cargoes which passed through the hands of the «pijnders» or dockers.

A memorial tablet on «De Rode Steen», a corner-house on the left of the Spiegelrei, commemorates Georges Rodenbach, the author of the famous novel «Bruges la Morte».

The Genthof, where the wooden gables have gradually disappeared since the 17th century on account of fire-risk, and the Wednesday Market (Woensdagmarkt) with its statue of Jan Memling, are passed on the way to the Oosterlingenplaats.

It was here that the powerful members of the German Hanseatic League from Cologne, Lübeck, Hamburg and other cities established their business houses. They contributed largely to the important role played by Brugge —together with London, Bergen and Novgorod— as a Hanseatic centre.

From the Spaanse Loskaai, where the Nation House of Castile among others was situated, you cross the Augustines' Bridge (1391) and turn left to the Vlaming Bridge. A handsomely restored brick oriel window, commissioned by the goldsmiths' guild and originally used as a smelting-furnace for gold, will attract your attention here. Across the bridge and righthanded through the Pieter Pourbusstraat, you now make your way to Saint James's Church.

This church, dating from 1240, came into its own in the 15th century thanks to generous gifts from the Dukes of Burgundy and foreign merchants. It was, however, yet another victim of the vandalism of the Iconoclasts (1580). Spectacular restoration work was carried out in the following two centuries, mainly in Baroque style.

It is only possible to give a short summary of the many art treasures on view here: the brass burial tablet of Catherine D'Ault; the monumental tomb of Ferry de Gros (treasurer of the Golden Fleece); an enamelled terra-cotta (Madonna and Child) by Della Robia; and noteworthy paintings by J. Van Oost, A. Cornelis and L. Blondeel. Along the St. Jacobstraat in the direction of the Market, you may turn left into the Naaldenstraat. The Bladelin Court, originally the home of Peter Bladelin — treasurer of the Golden Fleece and the Duke of Burgundy's chamberlain — came into the possession of the Medici family in 1466. Tomasso Portinari, Lorenzo de Medici's banking agent, took up his residence here and finally acquired possession of the building in 1480. A number of medallions in the courtyard walls portray some of its most famous inhabitants.

At the end of this street, turning right through the Kuipersstraat, you reach the Eiermarkt, where several colourful café terraces, in summer at least, invite you to take a breather. Here you meet once more the Bear of Brugge, proudly sculpted on top of the artistic stone pump which is a feature of this little square.

Kruispoort with historical museum.

Kruispoort (15th century).

*Windmill on the
Kruispoort rampart.*

The Ezelpoort.

A good place to begin a tour of folkloric Brugge is the Kruispoort. You can reach it on foot from the Market via the Breidelstraat, Hoogstraat and Langestraat.

Frequent bus services will drop you off there in a matter of moments.

Where the present Kruispoort now stands there were once two fortifications. Traces of their junction are still visible on the city walls which have since disappeared.

The building houses a museum providing a survey of over a century and a half of military history, the main accent being placed on the two world wars.

In addition to the Kruispoort, three other city gates — namely the Gentpoort, Ezelpoort and Smedenpoort — have been preserved almost intact. The remainder were systematically demolished under the rule of Emperor Joseph II in the 18th century.

A bronze skull has been inserted in one of the walls of the Smedenpoort, to commemorate the treachery of an inhabitant of Eeklo, who attempted to open the city gates to the occupier in 1691.

Not far from the Kruispoort, the air is cleft by the sails of three windmills. One of them, the St. Janshuismolen, is still in active service and can be visited and seen in full operation during the summer months. Marcus Gerards' plan, drawn in 1562, shows 25 mills on the ramparts, where the wind is caught to best advantage.

Birthplace of Guido Gezelle.

On the left of the first mill, in the Rolweg, stands the birthplace of Brugge's famous poet Guido Gezelle. Purchased by the Town Council in 1925, it is today a literary and didactic museum where the poet's life and work are on view. Several streetnames in this part of town bear witness to Gezelle's contemporaries such as Hugo Verriest, Albrecht Rodenbach and Stijn Streuvels.

You will also discover in the Rolweg the grounds and buildings of the Crossbow Archers' Guild of Saint George. One street further, in the Carmersstraat, is situated the building complex of the Saint Sebastian's Guild. Like their comrades-in-arms of the Saint George's Guild, this association's longbow archers formed part of the town militia in the middle ages. The emblem of Jerusalem in their coat of arms indicates that they also took part in the crusades.

Further down the Carmersstraat is the English Convent, where Guido Gezelle spent his last days.

Turning left through the Korte Speelmansstraat you enter the Balstraat.

Museum of Folklore.

Guido Gezelle (1830-1899) was born in one of the prettiest little streets in Brugge, the Rolweg. His birthplace is now a literary and didactic museum showing a panorama of the life and work of this great Flemish priest and poet.

GUIDO GEZELLE

A row of little houses, in which retired members of the cobblers' guild used to be lodged, has been restored and converted into the Museum of Folklore. Old-fashioned interiors have been tastefully reconstructed to include, among others, a sitting-room, an inn, a herbalist's shop and a pharmacy.

Across the street the Lace Centre (Kantcentrum) goes to great lenghts to keep up the centuries' old tradition of bobbin lacemaking, as well as adding a modern flavour to the classical designs. Here, regular courses and so-called «open lace days» are provided for enthusiasts who wish to master the deft art of manipulating lace bobbins.

The Jerusalem Church towers above both these groups of buildings. It is quite remarkable for its unique blend of highly diverse building styles.

The church, which has a Gothic substructure crowned by a bell-tower of oriental appearance, was built on the commission of the noble Italian Adorno family, who settled in Brugge in the 13th century. The plans for the church were based on those of the old Church of the Holy Sepulchre in Jerusalem, where various members of the Adorno family went on pilgrimage.

*Jerusalem
Church.*

When visiting this church, make a point of studying the magnificent stained-glass windows (1482), which are the oldest in Brugge; the monumental grave of Anselm Adorne and his wife; the white stone altar and calvary; and the crypt and Holy Sepulchre, which in conception and size is a faithful copy of the Holy Sepulchre in Jerusalem.

Next to the church there remain to this day six of the original twelve «godshuizen» for poor widows.

In the close vicinity, the spire of St. Anna's Church points towards the sky. This place of worship, where Guido Gezelle among others was baptized, has often been appropriately described as a «drawing-room church». Having been destroyed by the Beggar Protestants (Geuzen) in 1581, it was rebuilt, thanks to generous subscriptions by art-loving families, into a harmonious whole in which marble, copper, wood-carving and vaulting arches mutually complete one another.

In the Blekersstraat, a sidestreet of the Jeruzalem-straat, is to be found the oldest tavern in the town, namely the «Vlissinghe». In its old-fashioned 16th — 17th century interior you can pick up strength before resuming the last part of your walk.

The Blekersstraat runs into the St. Annarei; turning right and crossing the second bridge, through the St. Gilliskoorstraat, a sidestreet of the Lange Rei, you approach St. Giles's Church.

Museum of Folklore (Balstraat). Old Flemish kitchen.

It is an eloquent example of what is technically known as a «hall church» (three aisles of equal height). Famous painters such as Jan Memling, Lancelot Blondeel and Pieter Pourbus are thought to be buried either in the church or in the adjacent churchyard.

Back to the Lange Rei and over the next bridge, the Potterierei beckons to you.

The imposing buildings of the Episcopal Seminary stand in the place once occupied by the Abbey of the Dunes, originally founded in Koksijde, and whence the last Cistercians were expelled by the French regime in 1796.

Several works of art are housed in the Seminary, including a noteworthy collections of miniatures which unfortunately are not on view to the public.

Our Lady of the Potterie is a hospice founded in 1276, where old people are still taken care of. The buildings consist of a chapel and a museum with an incredible wealth of art treasures, including gold and silver chalices, monstrances, censers, etc.

The name «Potterie» commemorates the potters who had their chapel here. From the Lange Rei you can conclude your exploration with a bus-ride back to the Market.

Otherwise you may return along the Potterierei and the St. Annarei as far as the Blekersstraat, turn right over the bridge and take the second street to the left, which brings you to Saint Walburga's Church.

This church, consecrated to Saint Francis Xavier, has undergone the same turbulent history as the Jesuit order which vouched for its construction. After the abolition of the Order in 1779, it was granted the role of a parish church. During the French Revolution the church went through hard times, and was converted into a Temple of Reason. Notwithstanding its restless past, the church still harbours numerous pieces which are a testimony to its earlier glory: the pulpit sculpted by Quellinus the Younger, the communion rail, the magnificent choir, the statues of the apostles, etc.

Potterierei — «The Seven Plaguehouses».

This sanctuary once provided shelter for unfortunate women. The image of Our Lady of the Potters' Guild above the altar can be admired to this day: it has been venerated since the 13th century. Every year, on the eve of the Assumption of Our Lady the procession of Our Lady of the Blind sets forth from the neighbourhood of Brugge to light a candle here in devotion to Our Lady. This tradition originated during the wars of the 14th century, when Our Lady took the inhabitants of Brugge under her protection.
The Potterie Church also houses a museum containing attractive art treasures.

Saint Walburga's Church — Baroque style.

The Groene Rei.

A boat-trip along the canals is an ideal way to see the town. The pilots are expert guides, pointing out all the sites of interest to their passengers.

The above description of sites of interest can in no sense claim to be exhaustive. The imaginative visitor who leaves the well-beaten paths will certainly meet with many other surprising discoveries which will make his stay in Brugge an unforgettable experience.

Old wooden gable — near the St. Boniface Bridge behind the Church of Our Lady.

The 16th century Sluice House beside the Minnewater.

Groene Rei with (far right) «De Pelikaan» almshouse (17th century).

Bridge and entrance gate to the Princely Beguinage «Ten Wijngaarde».

Groene Rei.

The Groene Rei at night.

Trade flourishes in Brugge. Even under the arcades of the old Halles it's nice to shop among flowers and plants.

An excursion through Brugge in a horse-drawn coach has its charms too.

Pageant of The Golden Tree — The Burgundy-York float.

FOLKLORE

The folklore of Brugge is as wide-ranging and colourful as the history of the town itself. The Procession of the Holy Blood, which takes place annually on Ascension Day, is Brugge's most important folkloric event. More than two thousand people take part in this colossal pageant. The groups who accompany the relic of the Holy Blood portray Brugge during the period of her bloom. The whole town is bedecked with flags for the day, and converted as it were into an enormous stage on which the fame and glory of the past are represented.

Other spectacular events include the Carnival of Brugge, the May Fair and specially the Festival of the Canals: a show which takes place every three years. All kinds of attractive tableaux are enacted along the illuminated streets and canals.

We hope that you will enjoy and make the most of this splendid book, and that it will provide you with a permanently inviting memento and stimulating companion to the lovely town of Brugge.

Procession of The Holy Blood — Crusaders.

◁ *Procession of The Holy Blood — Proclamation.*

Procession of The Holy Blood — Clergy of Brugge with Shrine of the Holy Blood.

Procession of The Holy Blood — Virgin Mary, patroness of Brugge.

Pageant of The Golden Tree — Girls with coins.

Pageant of The Golden Tree — Float with Philip of Burgundy and Margaret of Flanders.

Pageant of The Golden Tree — Murder of Charles the Good.

Pageant of The Golden Tree — The beheading of the Giant of Mont Saint-Michel.

Along the Brugge-Sluis canal — windmill.

The Flemish landscape round Brugge is distinctly beautiful. In a varied countryside of woods, water, polders and farmland, midst quiet villages, castles and typical farms, is the setting of the town of Damme, home of the legendary Til Uilenspiegel.

Damme — Church of Our Lady.

Damme — Canal.

The proud tower of the Church of Our Lady rises from meadow and farmland, testifying to Damme's glorious past.

Town Hall — Damme. ▷

Little country chapel (1651).

TER DOEST ABBEY.

The monumental barn of Ter Doest Abbey in Lissewege is the only perfectly preserved part of the once famous and mighty Flemish coastal Abbey of The Dunes at Koksijde, whose restored ruins and museum are also well worth visiting. The small abbey chapel is to be found halfway between the village centre of Lissewege and the abbey barn. Turning right from the chapel, the visitor follows an alley of trees planted in the midst of delightful green pastureland to the former porched house of the abbey.

Exterior view of the monumental 13th century abbey tithe-barn.

Porched house (1662) of the former Ter Doest Abbey — now restored as a private house.

Entering the courtyard, with the great abbey barn on the left, one discovers the few remaining parts of the ancient abbey buildings. The well-known generosity and hospitality of the former lords of the abbey still reigns here, though nowadays it is given in return for a gladly paid financial sum. A wide variety of delicious country dishes is served in the Hof Ter Doest restaurant, whose charming interior owes much to the use of building materials from the former Ter Doest Abbey.

Interior view of the giant 13th century barn. The roof is still supported by the original solid wooden beams.

Collection ALL EUROPE

#	Title	Sp	Fr	En	Ge	It	Ca	Du	Sw	Po	Ja	Fi
1	ANDORRA	•	•	•	•	•	•				•	
2	LISBON	•	•	•	•	•					•	
3	LONDON	•	•	•	•	•					•	
4	BRUGES	•	•	•	•	•		•				
5	PARIS	•	•	•	•	•						
6	MONACO	•	•	•	•	•					•	
7	VIENNA	•	•	•	•	•		•			•	
8	NICE	•	•	•	•	•						
9	CANNES	•	•	•	•	•						
10	ROUSSILLON	•	•	•	•	•		•				
11	VERDUN	•	•	•	•	•		•				
12	THE TOWER OF LONDON	•	•	•	•	•						
13	ANTWERP	•	•	•	•	•		•				
14	WESTMINSTER ABBEY	•	•	•	•	•						
15	THE SPANISH RIDING SCHOOL IN VIENNA	•	•	•	•	•					•	
16	FATIMA	•	•	•	•	•				•		
17	WINDSOR CASTLE	•	•	•	•	•					•	
18	THE OPAL COAST		•	•	•							
19	COTE D'AZUR	•	•	•	•	•						
20	AUSTRIA		•	•	•							
21	LOURDES	•	•	•	•							
22	BRUSSELS	•	•	•	•	•		•				
23	SCHÖNBRUNN PALACE	•	•	•	•	•			•			
24	ROUTE OF PORT WINE		•	•	•			•				
25	CYPRUS		•	•	•			•				
26	HOFBURG PALACE	•	•	•	•	•		•				
27	ALSACE		•	•	•							
28	RHODES		•	•	•							
29	BERLIN	•	•	•	•	•						
30	CORFU		•	•	•	•						
31	MALTA		•	•	•	•						
32	PERPIGNAN		•									
33	STRASBOURG	•	•	•	•	•						
34	MADEIRA	•	•	•	•	•						
35	CERDAGNE - CAPCIR		•			•						

Collection ART IN SPAIN

#	Title	Sp	Fr	En	Ge	It	Ca	Du	Sw	Po	Ja	Fi
1	PALAU DE LA MUSICA CATALANA (Catalan Palace of Music)	•	•	•	•		•					
2	GAUDI	•	•	•	•	•					•	
3	PRADO MUSEUM I (Spanish Painting)	•	•	•	•	•					•	
4	PRADO MUSEUM II (Foreign Painting)	•	•	•	•	•						
5	MONASTERY OF GUADALUPE	•										
6	THE CASTLE OF XAVIER	•	•	•	•	•					•	
7	THE FINE ARTS MUSEUM OF SEVILLE	•	•	•	•							
8	SPANISH CASTLES	•	•	•	•							
9	THE CATHEDRALS OF SPAIN	•	•	•	•							
10	THE CATHEDRAL OF GERONA	•	•	•	•							
11	GRAN TEATRE DEL LICEU DE BARCELONA (The Great Opera House)	•	•				•	•				
12	THE ROMANESQUE STYLE IN CATALONIA	•	•	•								
13	LA RIOJA: ART TREASURES AND WINE-GROWING RESOURCES	•	•	•	•							
14	PICASSO	•	•	•	•							
15	REALES ALCAZARES (ROYAL PALACE OF SEVILLE)	•	•	•	•	•						
16	MADRID'S ROYAL PALACE	•	•	•	•	•						
17	ROYAL MONASTERY OF EL ESCORIAL	•	•	•	•	•						
18	THE WINES OF CATALONIA	•										
19	THE ALHAMBRA AND THE GENERALIFE	•	•	•	•	•						
20	GRANADA AND THE ALHAMBRA (ARAB AND MAURESQUE MONUMENTS OF CORDOVA, SEVILLE AND GRANADA)	•										
21	ROYAL ESTATE OF ARANJUEZ	•	•	•	•	•						
22	ROYAL ESTATE OF EL PARDO	•	•	•	•	•						
23	ROYAL HOUSES	•	•	•	•	•						
24	ROYAL PALACE OF SAN ILDEFONSO	•	•	•	•	•						
25	HOLY CROSS OF THE VALLE DE LOS CAIDOS	•	•	•	•	•						
26	OUR LADY OF THE PILLAR OF SARAGOSSA	•	•	•	•							

Collection ALL SPAIN

#	Title	Sp	Fr	En	Ge	It	Ca	Du	Sw	Po	Ja	Fi
1	ALL MADRID	•	•	•	•	•	•				•	
2	ALL BARCELONA	•	•	•	•	•	•					
3	ALL SEVILLE	•	•	•	•	•						
4	ALL MAJORCA	•	•	•	•	•					•	
5	ALL THE COSTA BRAVA	•	•	•	•	•	•					
6	ALL MALAGA and the Costa del Sol	•	•	•	•	•		•				
7	ALL THE CANARY ISLANDS, Gran Canaria, Lanzarote and Fuerteventura	•	•	•	•	•		•				
8	ALL CORDOBA	•	•	•	•	•	•				•	
9	ALL GRANADA	•	•	•	•	•	•				•	
10	ALL VALENCIA	•	•	•	•	•						
11	ALL TOLEDO	•	•	•	•	•						
12	ALL SANTIAGO	•	•	•	•	•						
13	ALL IBIZA and Formentera	•	•	•	•	•						
14	ALL CADIZ and the Costa de la Luz	•	•	•	•	•				•		
15	ALL MONTSERRAT	•	•	•	•	•	•					
16	ALL SANTANDER and Cantabria	•	•	•	•	•						
17	ALL THE CANARY ISLANDS II, Tenerife, La Palma, Gomera, Hierro	•	•	•	•	•			•	•		•
18	ALL ZAMORA	•	•	•	•	•						
19	ALL PALENCIA	•	•	•	•							
20	ALL BURGOS, Covarrubias and Santo Domingo de Silos	•	•	•	•	•						
21	ALL ALICANTE and the Costa Blanca	•	•	•	•	•		•				
22	ALL NAVARRA	•	•	•	•	•						
23	ALL LERIDA, Province and Pyrenees	•	•	•	•	•	•					
24	ALL SEGOVIA and Province	•	•	•	•	•						
25	ALL SARAGOSSA and Province	•	•	•	•	•						
26	ALL SALAMANCA and Province	•	•	•	•	•					•	
27	ALL AVILA and Province	•	•	•	•	•						
28	ALL MINORCA	•										
29	ALL SAN SEBASTIAN and Guipúzcoa	•										
30	ALL ASTURIAS	•	•	•	•							
31	ALL LA CORUNNA and the Rías Altas	•	•	•	•							
32	ALL TARRAGONA and Province	•	•	•	•							
33	ALL MURCIA and Province	•	•	•	•							
34	ALL VALLADOLID and Province	•	•	•	•							
35	ALL GIRONA and Province	•	•	•	•							
36	ALL HUESCA and Province	•	•	•	•							
37	ALL JAEN and Province	•	•	•	•							
38	ALL ALMERIA and Province	•	•	•	•							
39	ALL CASTELLON and the Costa del Azahar	•	•	•	•							
40	ALL CUENCA and Province	•	•	•	•							
41	ALL LEON and Province	•	•	•	•							
42	ALL PONTEVEDRA, VIGO and the Rías Bajas	•	•	•	•	•						
43	ALL RONDA	•	•	•	•							
44	ALL SORIA	•										
45	ALL HUELVA	•	•	•	•							
46	ALL EXTREMADURA	•	•	•	•							
47	ALL GALICIA	•	•	•	•							
48	ALL ANDALUSIA	•	•	•	•	•						
49	ALL CATALONIA	•	•	•	•	•	•					
50	ALL LA RIOJA	•	•	•	•							

Collection ALL AMERICA

#	Title	Sp	Fr	En	Ge	It	Ca	Du	Sw	Po	Ja	Fi
1	PUERTO RICO	•		•								
2	SANTO DOMINGO	•		•								
3	QUEBEC			•								
4	COSTA RICA	•		•								

Collection ALL AFRICA

#	Title	Sp	Fr	En	Ge	It	Ca	Du	Sw	Po	Ja	Fi
1	MOROCCO	•	•	•	•	•						
2	THE SOUTH OF MOROCCO	•	•	•	•	•						
3	TUNISIA			•	•							

The printing of this book was completed
in the workshops of
FISA - ESCUDO DE ORO, S.A.
Palaudarias, 26 - Barcelona (Spain)